Nineteen hundred and ninety six
things you wanted to know
about

WOLVERHAMPTON

Broadside

An initiative of

WOLVERHAMPTON PARTNERS IN PROGRESS

ACKNOWLEDGEMENTS

The information in this book is the copyright
of Wolverhampton Partners in Progress.

This book is printed on re-cycled paper.

ISBN 0 946757 09 7
Front Cover Photograph: Lichfield Street early 1900's
Front Cover Design: Malcolm Passant
Illustration Source: Peter Neald
Design and layout: Malcolm Passant

Published by
BROADSIDE
Studley House, 68 Limes Road,
Tettenhall, Wolverhampton, WV6 8RB
Telephone: (0902) 753047

WOLVERHAMPTON

LOCAL AUTHORITIES
Wolverhampton Metropolitan
Borough Council Civic Centre
(0902) 27811
Trading Standards Department
(0902) 312056

PUBLIC UTILITIES
Central Library (0902) 312025
The Post Office (0902) 875248
Postal and Telecommunications
Advisory Committee (0902) 773626
British Telecom (0902) 712712

GOVERNMENT OFFICES AND SERVICES
HM Customs and Excise
(0902) 771921
Department of Health and Social
Security
Wolverhampton North (0902) 311744
Wolverhampton South (0902) 22371

TRAVEL AND TRANSPORT
British Rail - Wolverhampton
(021) 643 2711
West Midlands Passenger Transport
Executive (0902) 351617

EDUCATION AND TRAINING
Wolverhampton Polytechnic
(0902) 313001
Bilston Community College
(0902) 353877
Wulfrun College of Further Education
(0902) 312062

LOCAL PRESS, RADIO AND TV
Express and Star (0902) 313131
Chronicle and Trader (0902) 313131
Wolverhampton Ad-News
(0902) 53506

Beacon Radio (0902) 757211
BBC Radio WM (0902) 311828
Central Television (021) 643 9898
BBC Pebble Mill (021) 414 8888

MISCELLANEOUS
Art Gallery and Museum(0902) 312032
The Grand Theatre (0902) 714775
Civic Hall (0902) 312031
Aldersley Stadium (0902) 751171
Citizens Advice Bureau (0902) 773626
Council for Community Relations
(0902) 713629
Wolverhampton Enterprise
(0902) 312095
Wolverhampton Information Centre
(0902) 312051
Wolverhampton Jobcentre
(0902) 772211
Manpower Services Commission
(0902) 49121
Skill Centre (0902) 27173
Careers Service (0902) 27811
Bilston Community College
(0902) 35387
Chamber of Commerce Training Unit
(0902) 26221
Wolverhampton Enterprise Ltd
(WELD) (0902) 312095/312096
Black Country Co-operative
Development Agency (0902) 312736
Department of Trade and Industry
(021) 632 4111
West Midlands Enterprise Board Ltd
(021) 236 8855
Training Agency (0902) 311111
Marketing Development Centre
(0902) 25130
Outset (Advice for disabled)
(0902) 20940
Wolverhampton Afro-Caribbean
Development Agency (0902) 24005

WOLVERHAMPTON'S MAJOR EMPLOYERS

Armitage Shanks Ltd (Bathroom fittings)	0902 733221

Chubb & Sons Lock and Safe Co Ltd (lock and safe manufacturers)	0902 55111

Fafnir Bearings Ltd (Metal Products)	0902 26101

GKN Sankey Ltd (Electronic and steel vehicle parts)	0902 43111

Goodyear (GB) Ltd (Manufacture and marketing of tyres)	0902 22321

James Beattie PLC (Six retail department stores throughout country)	0902 22311

Jenks and Cattell PLC (Manufacturers of garden tools)	0902 731271

Laystall Engineering Co ltd (Engineers)	0902 51789

Lucas Aerospace Ltd (Aerospace wing of Lucas Industries Group)	0902 782381

Manders Holdings PLC (Manufacturers of paint and retail property investment)	0902 53122

Marston Palmer Ltd (Aircraft components, atomic energy plant equipment)	0902 783361

Mitchells and Butlers Ltd (Beverages and Brewing)	0902 54551

NEI Thompson Ltd (Plant and systems for nuclear power industry)	0902 353353

Rockwell Automotive UK Ltd (Pressings for automotive industry)	0902 49213

Seamless Tubes Ltd (Metal products)	0902 305000

Spicer Transmissions Division (Transport equipment)	0902 771705

Tarmac PLC	0902 307407

Tarmac Construction Ltd	0902 22431

Tarmac Industrial Holdings Ltd	0902 41101

Tarmac Roadstone Holdings Ltd	0902 353522

Wednesbury Tube Company Ltd (Manufacture and supply of copper tubes)	0902 41133

Wolverhampton and Dudley Breweries PLC (Brewing and management of pubs and hotels)	0902 711811

Barclays Bank PLC	0902 22404

Birmingham Midshires Building Society	0902 710710

British Telecom PLC	0902 712712

SJ Dixon and Son Ltd (Merchants of paint and wallcovering)	0902 52491

Express and Star (Newspaper publishers)	0902 313131

First City Ltd (Land and Property consultants)	0902 712603

GKN Technology	0902 334361

Lloyds Bank PLC	0902 711617

Alfred McAlpine & Son Ltd (Construction)	0902 754151

Midland Bank PLC	0902 22481

Staffordshire Building Society	0902 772611

Wolverhampton Metropolitan Borough Council	0902 27811

Queen Square in 1760

PART ONE

910_AD_ _Areas of Wolverhampton thought to have been the scene of battle in which King Alfred's son, Edward the Elder's Saxon forces defeated the Danes._

966AD Probable founding of St Peter's Collegiate Church.

985AD Anglo Saxon King Aethelred "The Unready" made a grant of land at Heantun (High Town) - (Wolverhampton) to Lady Wulfruna, thought to be the sister of the old King, Edgar, who died in 976.

The area of land covered by the King's grant was bounded by Bilsatena (Bilston), Seeges League (Sedgley) and Tresel (Trysull).

994AD Lady Wulfruna made grant of land to the monastery of St Mary which stood where St Peter's Church stands today - the name Wulfrun Heatun first appeared.

In 1067 William the Conquerer granted the Collegiate Church with its lands and customs, to Samson, his chaplain and at the same time made him Bishop of Worcester.

Around 200 people lived in the area at the time of the Domesday Book,1086 including 14 slaves, six villagers, thirty smallholders and the churchmen and their families.

During the reign of King Stephen (1135-1154) reference to the name of Wulfrunhamton.

First mention of a market in 1179.

1180 The inhabitants ordered to pay a fine to Henry 11 for holding a market without a licence.

1204 King John took exception to the existence of a market without a royal charter.

On February 4th, 1258 King Henry 111 granted a charter for a market and fair to Lord of the Manor, Giles de Erdington, the Dean of Wolverhampton.

The charter gave the right of a weekly market to be held on Wednesdays and a fair to be held every year commencing on the vigil of the feast of St Peter and St Paul and to last eight days.

Valuations of the Deanery showed that in 1249 it was worth £25 and by 1291 was valued at £53.661/2pence

1332 taxation returns showed most of the inhabitants of the town were landowners and farmers.

During the reign of Edward 111 the people of Wolverhampton obtained the Grant of a Court Leet and Copyhold Court, known as the Deanery Court of Wolverhampton.

In 1465 the Deanery of Wolverhampton was annexed to that of Windsor.

The farmsteads of Wednesfield were heavily involved in the production of wool which comprised around 90 per cent of the exports of the whole country.

The "Old Hall" was erected around 1555 by the Levesons who continued to be resident in it until the reign of James 11. The building and estate were sold to the Earl of Bradford in 1684 and then it descended to the Pultney family. It was then let on lease to celebrated ironmaster John Turton giving it the name of "Turton's Hall".

COLLEGIATE CHURCH OF ST PETER

The Levesons were virtually the wealthiest family in the area, having prospered from the wool trade.   By the end of the 15th century the manor of Stowheath, which included parts of Bilston, Willenhall and Wolverhampton was almost totally in their hands.

Wolverhampton Grammar School was founded in 1512 by Sir Stephen Jenyns who was later to become Lord Mayor of London.

1560 and Richard Leveson was appointed High Sheriff for the County of Stafford.

Assizes held in the town for the trial of offenders within the parish.

The Collegiate Church first pewed in 1572 and the rood-loft removed.   It is thought that the galleries were erected at about the same time.

John Leveson founder and proprieter of the 'Old Hall" died in 1575.His remains, and those of his wife are entombed in the Leveson's Chancel.

In 1579 the plague caused many deaths in the town.

1590 was the date of the Great Fire which started in Barn Street (Salop Street) and destroyed 104 houses, 30 barns and a large quantity of grain.

The fire lasted for five days and left nearly 700 people homeless.

Thomas Smart and John Holyhead both charged with sheltering the Gunpowder Plot conspirators.

They were tried in Wolverhampton by a judge brought specially from Ludlow and executed in High Green (Queen Square) in 1606.

WASHING DAY A PLEASURE.

No Family need be without a

WASHING,

WRINGING,

AND

MANGLING

MACHINE,

When you can have one immediately by paying

1/6

PER WEEK

MACHINES

Delivered on First payment.

OLD MACHINES

Repaired or taken in Exchange for New Machines.

Warranted best Quality.

Liberal Discount to Cash Buyers.

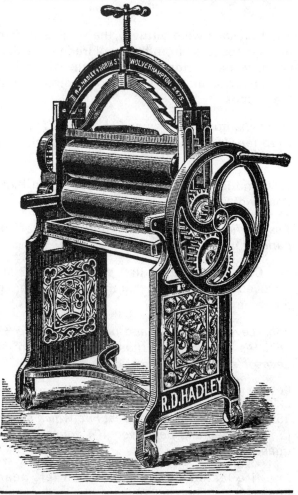

R. D. HADLEY & Co.,

9, North Street, Wolverhampton.

SEWING MACHINES, BEDSTEADS, AND PERAMBULATORS, ON EQUALLY EASY TERMS,

1610 the gallery for the Free Grammar School scholars was erected in the Collegiate Church by the Merchant Taylor's Company, London, trustees of the school.

Wolverhampton paid £72 Ship Money to Charles 1 - the rich paid more than the poor and sums varied from a shilling (5 pence) to about 37 1/2 pence.

Charles also raised £120 from Wolverhampton freeholders with a "knighthood fine".

When the Civil War broke out the great families of the area split with their loyalties and the Levesons and the Giffards fought with the Royalists and the Wrottesley's and the Lanes fought for Parliament.

The town in general was regarded as having Royalist sympathies. There were no battles or skirmishes in Wolverhampton although there were two garrisons in the town.

The first notable event in the Civil War in Wolverhampton was when Thomas Leveson called John Tanner a 'stinking rogue' and struck him about the head with a stick "making a great knob in the skin thereof".

Tanner was an armourer and he refused to return armour to Leveson because he knew he was a Catholic and a Royalist sympathiser.

In October, 1642 King Charles 1 on his way from Bridgnorth to Alston Hall stayed in Wolverhampton for three nights, accompanied by his two sons Charles, Prince of Wales and James, Duke of York.

In 1643 Prince Rupert visited the town and threatened to hang draw and quarter anyone between the ages of 16 and 60 who did not choose to fight for the King.

A Parliamentary force led by Sir William Brereton entered Wolverhampton early one morning in 1643 and , though they met no resistance, "captured it"

In June 1645 Charles was back in town and was given a bag of gold by a Mr Gough, who refused the reward of a knighthood. The knighthood was later conferred on his grandson by Charles 11.

The money was used to reward the army and each Colonel was presented with a 20 shilling piece in silver with all other officers receiving half a crown.

Sir William Brereton and Colonel Sanderson assembled a Parliamentary force of 1,800 infantry and 1,200 cavalry in the town.

Charles 11 found refuge in Boscobel, Moseley Old Hall and Bentley Hall after his defeat at the battle of Worcester in September 1651.

The Parliamentarians seized all Leveson's property including Bilston where the steward Will Tomkys went close to being killed for refusing to give any information about his master who had fled to Dudley Castle.

In 1655 the Deanery House was rebuilt.

The Leveson family left the area and the Goughs also left for their country seat at Bushbury.

Queen Square in 1820

13

On September 10, 1696 the second great fire in the history of Wolverhampton began , starting once again in Barn Street and within five hours 60 houses had been destroyed.

The total cost of the damage was estimated at £8,500.

In 1700 The Old Workhouse was erected at the top of Horseley Fields and the upper storey of the "Old Hall" was taken down.

The Old Meeting House in St John Street was erected in 1701.

In September, 1703 the inhabitants of Wolverhampton bought a fire engine and twenty four buckets for the water.

The engine was a box pump with a leather hose mounted on two wheels from which water was pumped out by half a dozen men, three on each side.

The Charity School was built in 1710 . By 1716 the staff were a master, paid £26 a year, a mistress paid £12 a year and a governess who was paid slightly more than £7 a year. Boys who were late for school would receive six strokes of the birch and girls would be whipped. Eight senior boys were appointed to report those who "cursed, swore, told lies or spoke unmannerly".

Reverend Thomas Moss author of the poem "The Beggar's Petition" was born in Wolverhampton around 1741.

Moss was the first curate of Brierley Hill Chapel of Ease, then became domestic chaplain to the Marquess of Stafford.

In 1743 Wheat sold in Wolverhampton market at 3 shillings (15pence) a bushel, barley and peas at 1/6 (7$\frac{1}{2}$p) and oats at 1 shilling and 2d a bushel.

A band of coiners was run out of the untenanted "Old Hall".

In 1750 a map produced by Isaac Taylor showed a cluster of houses around St Peter's Church and stretching out for some distance along the lines of the present main roads.

According to Taylor there were 1440 houses, and 7454 people in the town.

St James's Square, just off Horseley Fields was built around 1750. It consisted of a range of Georgian Houses, three storeys high.

The Square was the fashionable quarter occupied by the professional and employing classes who appreciated being close to the police and fire services.

Willenhall, Bilston and Wednesfield were allowed to bury their own dead in 1758 instead of taking them to Wolverhampton for interment.

1760 St John's Church consecrated.

The Birmingham Canal Navigation was completed in 1772.

1773 Mander, Weaver and Company's chemical works established in Cock Street.

At Tettenhall on September 1, 1776, James Brindley, most famous of all the canal engineers cut the first turfs in a field at Compton for the Staffordshire and Worcestershire Canal.

Celebrated tragedian John Kemble made his first debut on the Wolverhampton stage in the character of Theodoius in 1776.

In 1777 an Act of Parliament listed 125 residents of Wolverhampton as Commissioners responsible for the good order and governance of the town.

They were told to meet in the Red Lion for the benefit of their fellow citizens, authorised to levy rates and spend the money wisely and thriftily.

The commissioners had to be persons of substance with rateable property of £12 a year and £100 of real or personal estate.

The first regulations they issued included an order that a fine of 10s (50p) awaited anyone who washed brass dirt or ashes, or any kind of metal in the street.

Stallholders in the market place had to take down and carry away their standing before midnight on Wednesdays and Saturdays and before 10pm on any other day.

Scavengers had to organise a regular round for collection of ashes from houses and had to let the occupants know they were there by a bell or loud voice.

Bull or bear baiting was punishable by a fine of £5.

A £1 fine would be levied on anyone slaughtering an animal in the streets.

Property of the yearly value of £4 and not exceeding £7 was rated at 4d in the pound; £7 and not exceeding £14, 6d., and £14 and upwards 1s in the pound.

In 1778 John Kemble and his sister Mrs Siddons played in a large room on the upper storey of the Old Market Hall - the ground floor was used as a slaughterhouse.

In 1779 The Theatre was erected at the back of the Swan Hotel.

The Wolverhampton Chronicle was established in 1789.

1793 George Molyneux of North Street was appointed High Sheriff for the County of Stafford.

The town library was established in 1794.

Wesleyan Methodist Noah's Ark Chapel erected around 1795 - Wesley himself preached there.

In 1796 the price of wheat in Wolverhampton market had risen to 17/6 a bushel.

A watchman asleep in his 'watch-box' found himself being towed to London behind the coach after some young sparks had gently laid it down and tied it to the back of the coach.

The price of wheat in Wolverhampton market was 21s a bushel in 1800.

Street lighting in the form of an oil lamp at every corner and over the doorway of every Inn.

John Smith was paid 2/6d per street for painting the names in white lettering on black boards six inches high.

By turn of the century ten new wells had been sunk and a great water tank provided in the market place.

Householders, with the help of paupers from the poor house, had to clean the area in front of their houses every Thursday and Saturday.

By 1801 there were 2532 houses in the town and 12,565 inhabitants.

1802 - Union and Commercial Canal Wharfs and warehouses in Horseley Fields established about this time.

The Court of Requests was established in 1808.

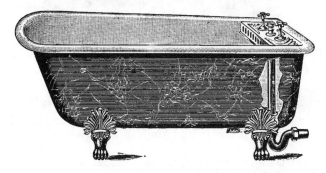

18

In 1811 the Dean of Wolverhampton empowered to grant licences for opening and working mines in the manor for any period not exceeding 50 years.

By the year 1812 there were 14,832 people living in the town in 2,935 houses.

Queen Street Chapel was erected around 1813 and the Union Flour and Bread Mill was established in Horseley Fields at a cost of £14,000.

Aaron Manby offered in 1817 to light the town with gas but the offer was refused by the Town Commissioners.

Town Improvement Act of 1814 banned the use of thatched roofing.

In 1818 building commenced of the south side of Queen Street and included the Mechanics Institute and the Dispensary.

Darlington Street was constructed on land bought from Lord Darlington for £350 an acre.

The street was built under the supervision of John 'Jack of all Trades' Worrallow who, as well as being town engineer was chief constable, sanitary inspector, weights and measures inspector and later became market manager.

By around 1819, 50 stage and mail coaches passed through the town every 24 hours.

In 1821 gas lighting was at last installed and to celebrate, a forty foot gas light column was erected in the Market Place on High Green.

Horse racing first established in the area in 1825 on the Broadmeadows Field where prize fighting also took place.

Cleveland Road finished in 1830.

1831 population of the town 24,732.

National Schools established in Cleveland Street.

Asiatic cholera ravaged Wolverhampton, Bilston, Tipton and surrounding country. Streets were cleaned and lime made available from a coach house owned by Mr Hills in Pigstye Walk.   The first case was a man who lived in Brickkiln Street and the whole number of reported cases was 578 with 193 deaths - many of whom were buried in St George's graveyard.

Town first enfranchised in 1832 and W.W. Whitmore and Richard Fryer were elected to the House of Commons.

The Grand Junction Railway opened its station at Wednesfield Heath - over a mile from the town centre - on July 4th, 1837.

Police Force first established in 1837.

Wolverhampton Water Works established in 1847.

On February 9th, 1847 a meeting was held to discuss Incorporation and before it was carried that the principle of local government be extended to Wolverhampton, a Mr Crane objected on the grounds that it would probably lead to an increase in the rates.

The first municipal elections took place on May 12th, 1848 and Mr Crane was one of the candidates .   He was elected and immediately appointed one of 12 Aldermen - a position he had criticised as an expensive luxury.

Thirty six councillors were elected from eight wards.

George Benjamin Thorneycroft elected first mayor of Wolverhampton.

The First Commission of Peace granted in 1849 and a Borough Bench of ten magistrates was set up with the Mayor as chief magistrate.

1853, March 9th: General Market first opened.

Oxford, Worcester and Wolverhampton Railway opened in 1854.

Great fire at Snow Hill, Griffin's and Garrick Street in 1857.

Library erected on Waterloo Road.

Widows of Wolverhampton send letter of sympathy to Queen Victoria on the death of the Prince Consort in 1861 and the Queen, deeply moved, said that if ever she appeared in public again it would be in Wolverhampton.

Dr James Glaisher and Henry Coxwell rose seven miles in a balloon ascent from Stafford Road Gasworksin 1862.

The Tettenhall College was opened in 1863.

Quarter Sessions court established in 1864.

1866 Queen Victoria kept promise to widows and visited Wolverhampton to unveil the statue of Prince Albert sculpted by Thomas Thorneycroft at a cost of £1,150. After the ceremony the Queen unexpectedely knighted the Mayor, John Morris and returned to the Railway Station to lunch on roast partridge, rabbit, boar's head , turkey, chicken, veal, oysters and ham.

1868 - The waterworks was aquired by the town and the system of deep sewerage works was begun.

Industrial exhibition opened by Earl Granville in 1869 was great success and raised £1000 profit.

The forerunner of the bicycle demonstrated and cycle racing before large crowds at the Molyneux Ground in 1870.

Town Hall built in 1871.

Wolverhampton Literary Club founded.

Population around 68,000 in 1871.

Circa 1870 first person summonsed for riding a bicycle on a public street. Mayor, as Chief Magistrate ruled that people had as much right to ride a cycle as a horse:"If they were foolish enough to do so."

One of the first towns to implement the Education Act of 1870 despite worries that :"working men will get into the town council" - and phrophesies of a revolution.

Old custom of "walking the Fair" when twenty four men dressed in antique armour, preceded by musicians followed by the Steward of the Deanery and principle citizens discontinued in late seventies by order of the Town Commissoners.

Fair abolished after becoming the haunt of the drunk and disorderly but restored again by Town Council six months later to placate angry populace.

Artisans Dwelling and Street Improvement Act applied after parts of town to East of St Peter's Church declared insanitary and unhealthy.

Fivepence halfpenny in the pound added to rates to pay for massive slum clearance scheme.

1888 - Wolverhampton became a County Borough.

Opening of Racecourse at Dunstall Park.

1889 Art gallery erected and presented to council by Philip Horsman.

1890 - committee formed to go into the matter of lighting the town by electricity.

Opening of Grand Theatre.

First Infectious diseases hospital opened.

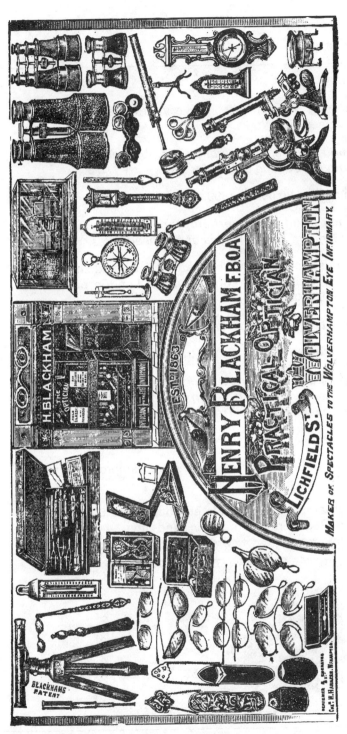

23

1896 - Opening of East Park. Five years later Lord Kelvin opened the Electricity Works.

1898 Borough celebrated its Jubilee and obtained grant of Coat of Arms from the College of Heralds.

Population around 90,000 in 1899.

1900 Council bought Wolverhampton Tram Company. Mr Alderman Mander fought the idea of overhead wires.

Arts and Industrial Exhibition opened by Duke and Duchess of Connaught and visited by Lord Mayor of London but closed with a loss of £30,000.

1902 Electricity Works makes first profit.

Six mile experimental electric tram track opened in 1902.

1904 - Motor bus company commenced running between Low Level Station and Bridgnorth. Corporation buses run for first time on the Lea Road route. Tram route extended to Bilston.

1905/6 tram route extended to Penn Fields.

Return of Colonel Thorneycroft and Wolverhampton Volunteers from Boer War.

1914 Wolverhampton Territorials embodied and 6th Bn South Staffordshire Regiment given a Civic send-off.

Zeppelins over Wolverhampton in 1916.

Lance Corporal Roland Edward Elcock won the Military medal and Victoria Cross for fearless behaviour.

Tank Week in the town raises nearly £1.5 millions - Gun Week another million.

1918 Thanksgiving Service in Market Place at end of World War 1.

November 23rd, 1918 War Minister David Lloyd George given Freedom of Borough and praised the people for their part in the survival of the Empire.

Earl Haig made Freeman.

Duke of York visited town, 1922.

1923 visit by Duke of Windsor.

Wolverhampton Corporation Act received Royal Assent on August 4,1926. Princess Mary opens technical school.

Queen of Spain visited Church of SS Mary and John , Snow Hill in 1927.   Earthquake felt in the town.

In 1927 Wolverhampton was the first town in the country to experiment with a system of traffic lights   It appears that following a visit of the Mayor to Germany to inspect lights, an experimental set suspended on wires and electrically controlled was installed in Princes Square on November 5, 1927. As the experiment was considered a success the first set of lights was permanently installed in Princes Square in October, 1928. The actual installation was not the first in the country because although Wolverhampton pioneered the project 9 months before any other town or city, both Leeds and Manchester installed sets first.

Prince George lay foundation stone of a Technical College.

In 1935 the only British town to take part in the Brussels International Exhibition and a Civic Deputation headed by the Mayor took a prominent part in "British Week".

Delegation from Baltic States entertained by Council and Chamber of Commerce.

Lord Dartmouth opened Corporation Civic Hall in 1938. Bantock House and Grounds bequeathed to the town by Alderman Baldwin Bantock.

To meet the war-time need for extra food around 4,500 temporary allotments were made available and cultivated in the town as well as the permanent 4,621 allotments.

A total of 16000 Anderson shelters were distributed during the war years.

1945 First Labour majority on town council.

Lord Woolton opened Wolverhampton of the Future exhibition.

Population in 1951 was 162,572.

Boundary re-organisation in 1965 made new population over 250,000

WOLVERHAMPTON
CORRUGATED IRON Co.,
SHRUBBERY IRONWORKS,
WOLVERHAMPTON.

ESTABLISHED 1857.

'*Emu Brand.*'

Galvanized, Corrugated, and Plain Sheets for Export.

Galvanized Iron, for Farm Sheds and Out-Buildings.

Water Tanks, Sheet Troughs, Corn Bins, Skips, &c.

PRICES ON APPLICATION.

"EMU BEST."

Collegiate Church of St Peter

Part Two

The prosperity of Wolverhampton in its formative years was based on WOOL, but with the approach of the Industrial Revolution the trade in the area gradually declined and moved to Yorkshire where Bradford became prominent in the trade.

Thanks to wool though the Leveson family was the richest in the area in the 15th century and by the end of that century they owned the manor of STOWHEATH which included parts of BILSTON, WILLENHALL and WOLVERHAMPTON.

The wealth amassed by some of the local families from the wool trade resulted in a major reconstruction programme for ST PETER'S CHURCH so that by the end of the 15th century the church had been converted to a cruciform plan, a clerestory was added and the tower was completed.

Much of the stone for the work was quarried from the ROCK on which the church was built.

It was the wealth from the woollen trade that resulted in the founding of the town's GRAMMAR SCHOOL in 1512. SIR STEPHEN JENYNS who had moved away from the town and settled in London to become a one time Lord Mayor and member of the Merchant Tailor's Guild did not forge his roots and provided the funds for the school building and the yearly interest on a further sum to pay for its running costs. The strong influence that wool had on the town was illustrated by place names such as FARMERS FOLD, MITRE FOLD and WOOLPACK ALLEY and the WOOLPACK on the Borough Arms. The place of wool was taken by the iron trade, after the discoveries of iron ore, coal and limestone along with plentiful supplies of timber.

In 1709 ABRAHAM DARBY succeeded in turning coal into coke for the smelting on iron at COALBROOKDALE, and just under 50 years later JOHN WILKINSON introduced coke at his BRADLEY FURNACE at BILSTON. He also used STEAM POWER to provide the blast for his furnaces and later, along with JAMES WATT and MATTHEW BOULTON, he ADAPTED THE STEAM ENGINE in the forge and rolling mill. WILKINSON was a LOCAL HERO and after his death local people gathered at MONMORE GREEN to wait for his GHOST to return.

During the 19th Century there were over 100 FURNACES in regular use in the area with NEW STEEL WORKS built by ALFRED HICKMAN in BILSTON which later became part of STEWART and LLOYDS

It was industries such as the making of LOCKS, SWORDS, BUCKLES, CHAINS, HINGES, LATCHES, POTS and PANS, COACH IRONWORK, PICKS and SHOVELS, AGRICULTURAL and MINING IMPLEMENTS that made the town famous throughout Europe.

FORGES were established at COVEN, BREWOOD, TRESCOT, FURNACE GRANGE, GREENSFORGE, SEDGLEY, COSELEY, BILSTON, WILLENHALL and districts to the East of the town.

Some of those industries survived and prospered, some weathered drastic changes and others died out as newer industry took over. For instance BUCKLE MAKING was unable to move with the changing fashions at the end of the Eighteenth Century. At the end of the 19th and beginning of the 20th Century such famous local names such as SUNBEAM cars and VILLIERS MOTORCYCLES appeared to be in a dominant position only to change later from the manufacture of complete vehicles to the making of components, including making parts for CONCORDE.

An important trade which was introduced early in the 18th century from Wales was the production of tinplate and japanned ware, which was found a home in TINSHOP YARD in CHARLES STREET and NORTH STREET. On SNOW HILL stood the OLD HALL erected by the LEVESON family in 1555 which had gradually become dilapidated and was leased for a tinplate and japan factory by JOHN TURTON.

The trade included the making of holloware finished in black and decorated in gold and colours. As tea was becoming a popular drink tea trays in sets were suitable presents for brides and there was a brisk demand for painters who could decorate them. In this way the town became well known for its group of ARTISTS of considerable skill.

One of them was EDWARD BIRD who was born at the back of CHEQUER BALL in OLD HORSEFAIR who painted coal scuttle lids for some years before he went to Bristol and established an art school.

JOSEPH BARNEY was another tea tray painter who is, however, better remembered for a large picture "The Descent from The Cross" which formed the reredos at ST JOHN'S CHURCH and by several other beautiful works which were preserved in the ROMAN CATHOLIC CHURCH in NORTH STREET.

CHARLES MANDER was a tinsmith and maker of what was known as Pontypoolware. His "Pontypool varnish" was so superior to that of his competitors that he was persuaded to sell his sheet metal business and concentrate on producing his varnish for other manufacturers.

Out of it grew the extensive business of MANDERS BROTHERS, manufacturers of all kinds of PAINTS, STAINS, PRINTING INKS and VARNISHES, while the name of MANDERS is linked with the heart of the present town in the title of the main shopping precinct, THE MANDER CENTRE.

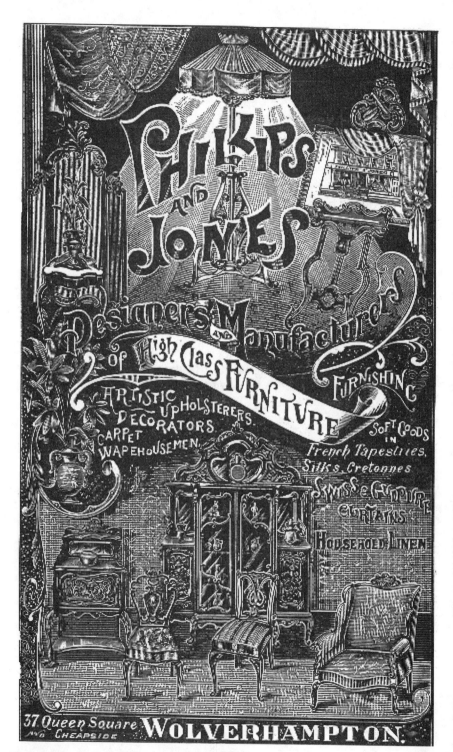

PHILLIPS AND JONES

Designers and Manufacturers of High Class Furniture Furnishing

ARTISTIC UPHOLSTERERS.
DECORATORS
CARPET
WAREHOUSEMEN.

SOFT GOODS IN
French Tapestries,
Silks, Cretonnes
SWISS & GUIPURE
CURTAINS
HOUSEHOLD LINEN

37 Queen Square and Cheapside WOLVERHAMPTON.

The sheet metal part of the business was bought by a Mr Schoolbread and Mr Loveridge who built a large factory in MERRIDALE STREET and trained their own artists at a SCHOOL of DESIGN at the corner of Darlington Street and what was aptly once named Art Street.

One useful sideline for the Japanners was the production of a paper made hardboard substance which was japanned in the same way as tinplate.

The first Nasmith steam hammer for the stamping of sheet metal goods was installed by Mr PINSON of PINSON and EVANS, DUDLEY ROAD, later incorporated in FORDHAM PRESSINGS and later known as FORDHAM PLASTICS LTD.

RICHARD and EDWARD PERRY constructed a large factory in TEMPLE STREET for the manufacture of sheet metal goods and Edward Perry also built DANES COURT at Tettenhall but did not survive to live there.

Danes Court was designed by architect CHARLES HANSOM who designed several other important Wolverhampton buildings including ST MARY and ST JOHN'S ROMAN CATHOLIC CHURCH on SNOW HILL.   But his real fame came from his invention and design of the HANSOM Cab which was made exclusively in the town by FORDRES of Cleveland Road.

JOHN MARSTON was a tinsmith and japanner who took up the manufacture of bicycles and made the famous SUNBEAM Cycle "with the little oil bath".

It is said, but cannot be substantiated, that the first Wolverhampton cycles were built around 1858 by one T. JOHNSON. The HART CYCLE COMPANY also claimed in their literature to have been cycle manufacturers since 1863.

Certainly the first of Wolverhampton's cycling fatalities occurred on October 9, 1869 when THE VALE OF EVESHAM NEWS reported that five friends were returning from practising at the Vauxhall Gardens, Cannock Road when, riding their Velocipedes along Pipers Row , one WILLIAM JONES, a carpenter swerved to miss a pedestrian and ran into a wagon, receiving such serious injuries that he died on the spot.

The cycle trade is believed to have thrown up the first occassion when WULFRUNA occured as a trade name with the production of an ORDINARY bicycle at the works of JOHN BARRATT, St John's Square.

Best known amongst the early bicycle makers was the firm of HENRY CLARKE who later founded COGENT CYCLES. After being wounded in the CRIMEAN war he returned to the family wheel-building business to concentrate on cycles and invalid carriages.   He launched Cogent Cycles from TEMPLE STREET wheel works in 1868 and became Wolverhampton's OLDEST CYCLEMAKER.

His premises were close to the TIGER'S HEAD public house owned by DAN RUDGE and the two worked together.   Clarke and Rudge had designed and developed an improved form of wheelbearing although it is said that they got the plans from a FRENCHMAN in the Tiger's Head whose tongue was loosened with copious amounts of Ale.

IN 1877 there were SIX principle makers of ORDINARY cycles as well as Dan Rudge and a number of smaller manufacturers. In 1878 the CYCLIST TOURING CLUB was founded. Henry Clarke produced a variety of Ordinary cycles throughout the 1880s when the better known of other makers were FRANK PARKYN of GRANVILLE STREET, S. GOODBY of MERRIDALE STREET, SHARRATT & LISLE of STEWART STREET and JOSEPH DEVEY of PIPERS ROW.

By late 1887 Wolverhampton had 15 manufacturers and within the next five years the highwheel Ordinary had been displaced. COGENT WORKS had to follow the trend and John Marston joined it toward the end of 1887. There was a growing demand for SAFETY cycles and the smaller machines reached an hitherto untapped market - that of WOMEN CYCLISTS. Dan Rudge's son and a partner called WEDGE went into business in 1891 with a works in MANDER STREET. In 1892 the CYCLE TRADE DIRECTORY numbered 59 CYCLE MAKERS in Wolverhampton. In 1898 Marston opened an Accessory Works "THE VILLIERS", in VILLIERS STREET.

But the boom had come to an end and manufacturers diversified - some into GENERAL ENGINERING and others into the expanding CAR and MOTOR CYCLE businesses. SUNBEAM and STAR founded the famous car companies and WERWELL, RUDGE-WEDGE and OLYMPIC , and later SUNBEAM made early motor cycles.

Into the 20th century it was the name of Sunbeam that became and remained the town's famous cycle maker. A COUNCILLOR and former MAYOR of the town, John Marston, true to his traditions as a VICTORIAN craftsman set out to make the FINEST CYCLE in the country. "THE GOLDEN SUNBEAM" was five or six times the price of ordinary bicycles and it was finished in BLACK ENAMELLED and lined in real GOLD LEAF.

Its basic design with a chain enclosed by a CARTER chaincase lasted from the 1890's to the 1950's and after 1937 was made by AMC of London , BSA and Raleigh. The famous badge was put on child's cycles where it REMAINS today. The industry was in decline after World War Two and in the early 1970's the last WEARWELL factory was bought by ELSWICK HOPPER.

Meanwhile the town had become world renowned for the motor cycles it made and it is thought possible the FIRST MOTORCYCLE made in England was built by the STEVENS BROTHERS when they fitted an American MITCHELL ENGINE to a WEARWELL CYCLE during 1897.

Motorcycles made in the town went on to win success in EVERY BRANCH OF COMPETITION - RACING, TRIALS and SPRINTS RECORD BREAKING and at one time AJS were making 25,000 bikes a year.

The first AJS appeared in 1911 made at RETREAT STREET and later at GRAISLEY. The AJS won the ISLE OF MAN junior TT four times, THE SENIOR once and the LIGHTWEIGHT once.

The company however was liquidated in 1931 but during 1934 the STEVENS BROTHERS started again at the RETREAT STREET WORKS and produced the 'Stevens' motorcycles and light commercial vehicles.

As with all John Marston products the SUNBEAM MOTOCYCLES introduced during 1912 were of very high quality and they were expensive. The 1920 $3\frac{1}{2}$hp solo cost £180 and sold to the slogan "THE GENTLEMANS MOTORBICYCLE". Sunbeam won, FOUR Senior TTs, and four Manufacturer's TEAM prizes in sprints ridden by GEORGE DANCE. Marston's sold out just ater World War One but Sunbeams were made at SUNBEAMLAND until 1937 when production was moved to Plumstead.

Chas. W. Harness,

Designer & Illustrator

WOOD ENGRAVING IS UNDOUBTEDLY THE BEST MEANS OF ILLUSTRATING CATALOGUES

ESTIMATES for every description of ILLUSTRATING sent Free BY RETURN of POST

Engraver on WOOD or COPPER PLATE, BRASS, &c.

Princes Chambers, Princes Square, WOLVERHAMPTON

Catalogues Illustrated

WITH

WOOD BLOCKS,
PHOTO PROCESS BLOCKS,
OR COPPER PLATE.

EFFECTIVE ADVERTISEMENT BLOCKS

Designed and Engraved at very cheap rates.

BRASS PLATES for Doors, Gates, and Shop Fronts.

Memorial Brasses

Designed and Engraved in elegant style.

Rubber Stamps, Visiting Cards. . . . .
. . . *General Engraving of every description.*

Prince's Chambers, Prince's Square, WOLVERHAMPTON.

37

CLYNO of THRAPSTON, who had been engine customers of STEVENS moved to PELHAM STREET WORKS in 1909 and started to produce a 'V' TWIN SIDECAR model and during World War One around 1800 were built and used as MACHINE GUN CARRIERS. The company struggled on after the war but during 1922 decided to concentrate on the production of CARS.

The popular DIAMONDS were first made at SEDGLEY STREET and one of the founders of the company also designed the OMEGA motorised cycle made in ST JAMES' SQUARE in 1908/9. Dorsett was also responsible for the ORBIT made from 1919 to 1924. Later Diamonds were made in VANE STREET and used a variety of engines including Barr & Stroud, Villiers and JAP and around 1926 prices ranged from £29 to £57. Diamond closed down in 1932 after competing in several TT races and coming a best seventh in the 1926 LIGHTWEIGHT race.

HOWARD R. DAVIES who had enjoyed a successful competition career with AJS decided in 1924 to set up as a manufacturer in HEATH TOWN, soon moving to FRYER STREET. The fine if expensive machines became world famous and in 1926 Davies was able to claim the WORLD'S FASTEST 500cc motorcycle, having acheived 104mph.

Sales fell and during 1928 the company sold out.

During 1901 Wearwell began making motorcycles in GREAT BRICKLIN STREET under the WEARWELL, WOLF and WULFRUNA trademarks and remained in production until 1939 when the were by then being made by the WAIN family at works in COLLIERY ROAD.

STAR were not prominent as motorcycle manufacturers and what they did offer faded out after World War One. EFFICIENT ENGINEERING in Bilston Road was run by T.C. JUCKES who had built motorcycles from 1902. Between 1920 and 1925 when the company was liquidated he offered a range of two strokes and an overhead valve model with a top speed of 80mph at £54.

H.B. MACHINES which were only in production for three years were made in WALSALL STREET by HILL BROTHERS. The first motorcycle made by FRANK PARKYN appeared in 1902 and after he enjoyed some success at his works in GRANVILLE STREET production ceased in 1923.

VILLIERS started making engines in 1911 but it was the two-stroke introduced during 1913 and the FLYWHEEL MAGNETO that brought worldwide fame to the company. As suppliers to many manufacturers the company did not offer a complete machine but PETER INCHLEY constructed some racing machines under the Villiers name and in the 1966 LIGHTWEIGHT TT he came third - the first time a British machine had been in the first three for 16 years.

The town also became world famous for the cars and commercial vehicles produced. Quality vehicles were made by Sunbeam and Star and Clyno offered a good mass produced car. Great PRESTIGE was brought to the town by Sunbeam by building the FIRST CAR to exceed 200 mph - and the CAR THAT WON the FRENCH GRAND PRIX.

The first Star car based on the Benz emerged in 1899 with a 3 1/2hp water cooled motor and the following year a twin cyclinder car became available. In 1905 the STARLING was being sold for £110 and Star were also selling their first commercial vehicles. In 1907 the FIRST six cylinder STAR was made and by 1911 the company were among the SIX LARGEST in the country. In 1928 the company was taken over by GUY MOTORS who continued to make Stars until 1932. Malcolm Campbell spent some time at the wheel of a Star. The first real Sunbeam car was the 1903 12 hp based on the French Berliet with a chain drive and the famous "little oil bath". In 1905 only about TWENTY people were employed making around 130 CARS a year. The turning point in the fortunes of the company occurred in 1909 when Frenchman LOUIS COATLEN was apointed chief engineer. He soon had Sunbeams racing at BROOKLANDS and in 1912 three Sunbeam three litre cars were entered for the COUPE DE LA AUTO and won first THREE PLACES.

In 1923 Henry Seagrave won the FRENCH GRAND PRIX in a Sunbeam- the first time a British car had finished first. More successes followed and Seagrave became the FIRST to EXCEED 200mph on land.when he drove the 100 hp Sunbeam at Daytona during 1927 and was KNIGHTED for the achievement. In 1919 the quality 16hp Sunbeam cars sold for £790.

In 1920 Sunbeam became part of the SUNBEAM, TALBOT DARRACQ group and by 1926 a straight eight was offered for £1,975. The approach of 1930 saw a fall in demand for expensive cars and a 1930 "DAWN" saloon on sale at £485 was a failure. Sunbeam production which had included some commercial vehicles and trolley buses closed down after a takeover in 1935 by a subsidiary of Rootes.

The first Clyno's had 14hp Coventry Climax engines and 500 were sold for £250 in the first year. By 1926 they were producing 300 a week and a new factory was built at BUSHBURY in 1927. A price war led to Clyno's downfall and in an attempt to compete with the Morris Minor the company produced the CENTURY which cost only £115 but attracted few buyers.

Guy Motors, founded in 1914 by SIDNEY GUY at FALLINGS PARK won fame for commercial vehicles and buses but also made about 150 V8 luxury cars and a few small four cylinder models.

A new factory was built in WALSALL STREET to house the production of BRITON cars which was founded in 1909. During 1922 the company fell into financial difficulties and was taken over by CHARLES WEIGHT of SEBCO. A further 1000 cars were produced before the firm turned to tractor spares and in 1929 car production was halted. TURNERS MOTOR MANUFACTURING COMPANY was offering what was claimed to be the FIRST LIGHT PETROL MOTOR in 1908 but after some success the firm failed to recover from the War years and finally ceased production in 1928. AJS entered the car market in 1930 with closed and open models priced from £210-240 - too expensive - and the design was taken over by Crossley Motors when the company was liquidated. Some sports cars were produced during the 1950s by CYRIL KIEFT at works in DERRY STREET and after he ran a car in the 1954 Le Mans 24 hour race he sold replicas for £1,560. Jack Turner with works on Pendeford airport produced sports cars for a time.

WOLVERHAMPTON'S LOCKSMITHS have always been amongst the most experienced craftsmen in Europe. At first they worked in wood and the principles of the craft formed the basis for the raw materials of iron and bronze. A trade directory compiled in 1770 mentioned 24 different types of locks and in 1855 WILLENHALL contained the premises of 340 locksmiths, Wolverhampton 110 and BILSTON 2.

The New Post Office

The name of CHUBB is renowned throughout the world. They invented the DETECTOR LOCK, and produced high quality LEVER locks of outstanding quality during a period of 140 years. In 1818 the Detector lock was patented by Jeremiah Chubb and he was rewarded by the government for the production of a lock that could not be opened by any other than its own key. A story goes that a convict on board a prison ship in Portsmouth Dockyard heard of the lock and thinking that he was capable of picking it accepted a challenge from Mr Chubb who offered a £10 reward if he could do it. The story has it that the government even offered a pardon if the convict was successful. He spent two or three months trying to pick the lock but gave up saying that Chubb's were the most secure locks he had ever known and that it was impossible to pick them with false instruments. After such a TESTIMONIAL is was natural that Chubb should have thrived. The fate of the convict is unknown.

The CANALS of Wolverhampton are now the target of the leisure industries and conservationists but, of course, it has not always been so.

In 1766 JOHN PERRY called a meeting in the town to organise backing for a canal to connect the Severn and Trent and to serve Wolverhampton. It was to become known as the Staffordshire and Worcestershire Canal

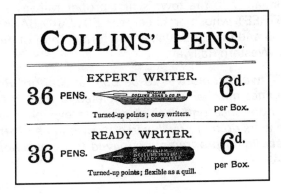

The S and W Canal followed the valleys of the PENK, the SMESTOW and the STONE but it proved impossible to get very close to the town so from 1770-1772 COMPTON was the terminus and goods had to be taken overland.

By November 1770 the Birmingham Canal was near BILSTON and the S & W Company tried to compel the BCN to complete a promised connection. The link was made on SEPTEMBER 21st, 1772 at ALDERSLEY although the Birmingham Canal had to fall 125 feet to join S & W. It was first proposed to make 40 locks but the design was altered to one of 19 with a six foot drop and one of 12 feet although the last fall was later split into two six feet locks to give the 21 locks that remain. Builder JAMES BRINDLEY died a week after the link was made.

At one time Wolverhampton boasted several railway stations, including the two important ones near to the town centre, THREE locomotive depots and a major railway works, The STAFFORD ROAD WORKS known as the "Factory" of the Great Western Railway. The FIRST Railway to serve the town skirted the centre on its way from Warrington to Birmingham. The GRAND JUNCTION RAILWAY opened its station at WEDNESFIELD HEATH on July 4, 1837. The second railway - The Shrewsbury and Birmingham opened a temporary station in November 1849. The Stour Valley Railway commenced at a junction with the Grand Junction Railway at Bushbury and climbed steadily to the town's first proper railway station on QUEEN STREET whose architect was EDWARD BANKS. The new station and the Stour Valley line formed part of the London and North Western Railway.

The FIRST two locomotives to be built at Stafford Road were tender engines number 7 and 8 completed in 1859. The works grew in importance until lack of space to expand meant more and more work going to rival works at Swindon and after a mid-thirties rebuilding programme survived to repair engines until June 1964.

Big changes came in the 1960s when London Midland Region took over all lines and the ex LMS line through High Level was electrified as part of the Euston to Glasgow electrification. After March 1967 all inter city services used High Level and the importance of Low Level Station declined so that the LAST local passenger trip to Birmingham Snow Hill took place on March 4, 1972.

FAMOUS AND INFAMOUS.

Thomas Parker of Tettenhall invented Coalite in 1905 and built a plant for its production in Wednesfield - but the invention was unsuccessful until the Clean Air Act of fifty years later. He also made outstanding improvements in connection with electrical engineering including developments in storage batteries. The Elwell Parker Dynamo was a big advance on its predecessor and his work on electrictraction led to the development of the tramcar and the London Underground.

Sir Richard Leveson served as a volunteer under Sir Francis Drake on the Ark Royal in 1588 and took part in the defeat of the Spanish Armada. Knighted in 1596, given the title 'Vice Admiral of the Fleet' in 1603 and went to Madrid as a member of the delegation which concluded the peace between England and Spain.

Button Gwinett was born in 1735 at Down Hatherley in Gloucestershire and came to Wolverhampton as a young man to work for Aaron Bourne, a tea merchant who had a shop in Lych Gates. He married the boss's daughter Ann and they had three daughters. In a hurry to get rich he went to America where he became the first governor of Georgia and his name has second place on the list of signatories of the Declaration of Independence. His signature is prized by collectors.

Edwin Booth, well known for his painting and for his ability as an actor which he displayed at the theatre at the rear of the Swan Inn on High Green (now Queen Square) deserted his wife and went to America where his son Wilkes Booth assassinated President Lincoln.

Sir Charles Marston was the eldest son of the founder of the Sunbeam Cycle and motor car companies and was eventually put in charge of the Villiers Cycle Components Company in Villiers Street. He did sterling work for charity.

John Wilkinson was known as "Ironmad Wilkinson" and built the first steam powered blast furnace at Bradley Ironworks, Bilston and also helped in the construction of the "Iron Bridge" which was caste at Coalbrookdale. At one time he offered to pay off the National Debt. He was buried in an iron coffin.

Jonathan Wild was born in Wolverhampton in 1683 but moved to London where he became famous as a dealer in stolen property and organiser of gangs of thieves. He called himself "Chief Thieftaker General of Great Britain" a nickname earned by informing on other criminals. He was, however executed on May 24,1725.

Sir Henry Hartley Fowler became MP for the town in 1880 and was made the first Freeman of the Borough. In 1894 he became Secretary of State for India, a position that saw him decorated with the Order of the Grand Commander of the Star of India by Queen Victoria.

Moses Ironmonger was Mayor from 1857-8 and 1868-9 but is remembered for having been a friend of Alexander Graham Bell, inventor of the telephone and is said to have received from Bell the first recorded public telephone call in 1867.

Councillor Samuel Griffith built Whitmore Reans Hall at about 1850 but in 1857 he went bust for £160,000 and it is said that the high wall he built around the Hall was to keep his creditors out.

Wolverhampton Orphan Asylum.

Sir Charles Villiers was a member of Parliament for 63 years from 1835-1885 as the sole Member for Wolverhampton and then from 1885 until his death in 1898 as MP for Wolverhampton South.

Sir Charles Wheeler was the first sculptor ever to be elected President of the Royal Academy of Arts. Born in Codsall in 1892 he first studied at the Wolverhampton School of Art and later at the Royal College of Art. He sculpted the statue of Lady Wulfruna which stands outside St Peter's Church.

Other examples of his work can be found in the Bank of England, India House and South Africa House.

Dame Maggie Teyte was one of the greatest opera singers of the 20th century. Her father owned the Old Still Inn in King Street. Maggie was sent to the Royal College of Music and later to Paris to study under Jean de Reszke. In 1908 she was selected to sing the title role Melisande at the Opera de Commique in Paris - a role which was the beginning of an opera career which lasted nearly 60 years.

Poets Sir Henry Newbolt (1862-1938) and Alfred Noyes (1880-1958) were born in the town as was John Abernethy, FRCS (1764 - 1831) who became President of the Royal College of Surgeons.

PART THREE

IN the 1890s a labourer in Wolverhampton would expect to earn 15 shillings (75p) a week and a nail maker or chain maker about £1 a week. Engineering workers, carpenters and builders wages for a 54 hour week were in the region of £2, whilst a furnace foreman might get £3 a week for 60-70 hours.

Outgoings for the basic requirements of life were typically: Rent 4/6 (22½p), a week for a four bedroomed house; Bread 3¾d (2p) per 4 lb loaf; Butter 10¼d(4p) a pound, Beef 5d (2p) per pound and Ale 9d (4p) a gallon.

PROMOTIONS and sponsorship by business and industry is nothing new. In 1898 Nestles Milk and Sunlight Soap promoted a display of animated photographs at the Exchange Hall in Exchange Street of the great test match between England and Australia supported by a variety bill which included a Mexican "double voiced nightingale" Mdlle Esmeralda,George Egbert (Premier siffleur) and Zingari and Bartoni (Living Statuary).

THEATRES in Wolverhampton became "in the fashion" and adopted a twice nightly system of shows in 1900. The system had been pioneered in Chatham to cater for Naval Officers and Ratings.

Empire Theatre prices in June, 1900 were stalls 1/6d (7½p), Circle 1/- (5p), Pit 6d (2½p), Gallery 4d (1½p) and Circle 9d (4p).

Harry Lauder appeared in Wolverhampton at the Hippodrome Theatre on October 29, 1906.

The Wolverhampton Empire which opened in 1898 played host to most of the stage stars of the day. A regular was George Beauchamp whose successful songs were "She was one of the Early Birds" and "Get your hair cut!". Mark Sheridan had many successful songs including "I do like to be beside the seaside" later adopted as his signature tune by Reginald Dixon at Blackpool's Tower Ballroom.

Jack Pleasants sang "I'm shy Mary Ellen" and "Twenty One Today" and Charles Whittle's "Let's All Go Down The Strand" was popular.

George Formby was billed as "The Lancashire Lauder" and Harry Champion sang about "Boiled Beef and carrots". Charles Coburn of "Two Lovely Black Eyes" fame appeared in 1916 but recalled a previous engagement in Wolverhampton Music Hall in 1878.

It is thought that an act at the Empire on July 31st, 1899 - "Eight Lancashire Lads",included 10 year old Charlie Chaplin.

The Fred Karno Troupe first appeared at the Empire in 1899.

Harry Houdini first appeared at the Empire in 1905 and told the audience that he had asked but been refused permission to escape from a police cell below the Town Hall.

One of the last revues at the Empire was "Mr Tower of London" and starred Gracie Fields. Five weeks later the Empire theatre closed - the final show was a revue called "Short and Sweet".

Charles Dickens appeared at the Exchange Theatre in 1851.

Films were first shown in the town at the turn of the century at the Friar Ground.

The first cinema was the Electric Theatre in Queens Square, opened on January 24, 1910.

THE GRAND THEATRE

Stars who appeared at the demolished Hippodrome included Billy Cotton and His Band, Big Bill Campbell and His Hometown Mountain Band, Joe Loss and His Band, Max Miller, Anne Shelton,Sandy Powell and Jessie Matthews.

The final act of the Gunpowder Plot took place near to Wolverhampton at Holbeache House in Himley where a number of the conspirators including Robert Catesby had hidden. Two other men named Thomas Smart and John Holyhead of Rowley Regis were charged with sheltering the plotters and were tried in Wolverhampton by a judge brought specially from Ludlow. They were executed on High Green (Queen Square) on, or about January 27, 1606.

Prime Minister David LLoyd George received the Freedom of the Borough on November 23rd 1918 and at the Grand Theatre he made the speech which contained the famous phrase "a country fit for heroes to live in".

St Peter's Church was first broadcast on the radio on Jauary 17, 1937.

A captured Messerschmitt aircraft was put on display outside the Molyneux, North Street, on October 21, 1940.

Cinemas opened on Sunday for the first time on April 27, 1941

The first prefabricated house was occupied in late 1945.

The lake in West Park took boats for the first time in July, 1949.

The Airport hosted the King's Cup Air Race which included Group Captain Peter Townsend in his Hurricane in 1950

The Central Fire Station was built in Red Lion Street in the early 1850's when the Brigade was voluntary.

The Fire Brigade came under the control of the police in 1890 when the equipment was a one hose handcart and a mechanical fire extinguisher.

Two Dennis Motor turbine pumps replaced the Fire Brigade's single horse drawn steam engine in 1914.

The first recorded parking offence for the town was December 13, 1826 when a driver left his horse and cart unattended.

The Royal Hospital, Cleveland Road was originally the Wolverhampton and South Staffs General Hospital erected between 1846 and 1848 at a cost of £18,000.

The King George's Memorial Wing was added in 1912.

Jack Hawkins starred in the film "The Man in the Sky" when action shots were produced at Wolverhampton Airport in 1950.

Princess Margaret visited Heath Town on April 2, 1969.

The Queen visited Wolverhampton in 1962.

In 1910 the Midlands Aero Club held its first flying week at Dunstall Park racecourse attended by A.V. Roe, the designer and maker of AVRO aeroplanes.

The Collegiate Church of St Peter stands at the highest point in the town.

The font was carved in about 1480 and the stone pulpit was given in about 1450.

The Jacobean Altar in The Lady Chapel is thought to have been consecrated by Archbishop Laud in 1635.

The town celebrated its millennium in 1985.

The County Courts Building was originally the Assembly Room and Library, the Town Council first met there in May 1848.

Queen Square in 1867

The Art Gallery and Museum was designed by J.A. Chatwin and built in 1884.

Wolverhampton's Dunstall Racecourse was opened in 1888. The course made history in 1962 by staging Britain's first Saturday night race meeting.

Eight Tipton workmates smashed the world record for a pools win when they shared more that £1.5 millions from Littlewoods in August 1990.

Wolverhampton lorry driver Trevor Carless apeared in a TV blockbuster Onassis - The Richest Man in the World after being spotted on holiday with his family in Majorca.

Wolverhampton company Tarmac was one of ten companies involved in the Channel Tunnel project.

Mrs Marj Horton of Tettenhall, a member of the British Chelonia Group - a conservation group aimed at protecting shell-bearing species, breeds tortoises in her airing cupboard.

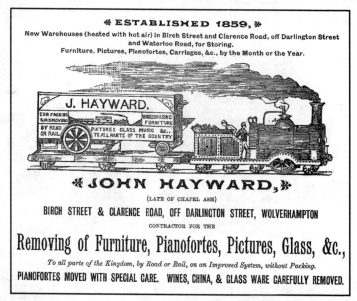

❋ **ESTABLISHED 1859.** ❋

New Warehouses (heated with hot air) in Birch Street and Clarence Road, off Darlington Street and Waterloo Road, for Storing.
Furniture, Pictures, Pianofortes, Carriages, &c., by the Month or the Year.

J. HAYWARD.

❋ **JOHN HAYWARD,** ❋

(LATE OF CHAPEL ASH)

BIRCH STREET & CLARENCE ROAD, OFF DARLINGTON STREET, WOLVERHAMPTON

CONTRACTOR FOR THE

Removing of Furniture, Pianofortes, Pictures, Glass, &c.,

To all parts of the Kingdom, by Road or Rail, on an Improved System, without Packing.

PIANOFORTES MOVED WITH SPECIAL CARE. WINES, CHINA, & GLASS WARE CAREFULLY REMOVED.

PART FOUR

A great diversity of trees, plants and wildlife occurs within the environs of the town - in the gardens, woodlands and open spaces.

Wolverhampton is particularly fortunate in that it has many miles of canals and disused railway track providing ideal conditions and homes for birds, animals and plants.

At the PENDEFORD NATURE RESERVE for instance the WATER FERN has become established.   That was introduced by man but the British wild plants form an impressive array in the remnants of the countryside around and in the town.

The older woodlands contain WOOD SORREL, SLENDER FALSE, BROOM, WOOD CLUB-RUSH, AND WOOD ANENOME.

Several species which are scarce in the West Midlands, for instance the TAWNEY SEDGE and BOG PIMPERNEL can be found on PENN COMMON and THE GORGE and SEDGLEY BEACON play host to lime loving plants.

The town has two species of Oak, THE ENGLISH OAK and THE TURKEY OAK which can be found on DUNSTALL HILL.

THE TRAVELLER'S JOY occurs around TETTENHALL and near LADYMOOR POOL in BILSTON.

LESSER KNAPWEED and GREATER KNAPWEED can be found in the limestone areas of SEDGLEY BEACON with COMMON MILKWORT and CARLINE THISTLE and at HORSELEY FIELDS.

OXFORD RAGWORT thrives in the heart of the town and the BOGBEAN normally found in upland pools and swampy ground has been found in a ditch on PENN COMMON along with the even rarer FEW FLOWERED SPIKE-RUSH. The FLOWERING RUSH grows along some canals and the SLENDER RUSH - an alien from NORTH AMERICA has been found growing at LADYMOOR.

More than 60 SPECIES of birds have been recorded as nesting in the area since 1970. The CANADA GOOSE nests regularly on lakes in WEST PARK and the BLACK HEADED GULL has colonised CRANMERE BOG and also roosts on CHILLINGTON POOL and BELVIDE RESERVOIR along with HERRING GULLS, COMMON GULLS and BLACK-BACKED GULLS. A rare ARCTIC bird the ICELAND GULL has been seen on a rubbish tip at WEDNESFIELD.

KESTRELS nest throughout the area and SPARROW HAWKS appear regularly on the edge of town.

The Summer visitors, SWIFTS, SWALLOWS and HOUSE MARTINS occur in profusion and THE GREATER SPOTTED WOODPECKER is a regular visitor in Autumn and Winter and one has been seen in ST PETER'S GARDENS outside the art gallery. THE GREEN and LESSER SPOTTED WOODPECKER also occur in the town and are most likely to be seen at TETTENHALL and WIGHTWICK.

Even the NUTHATCH has been seen in PENN and BANTOCK PARK.

The propensity to plant conifers in gardens has led to the presence in may gardens of the GOLDCREST and its tiny, much scarcer relative the FIRECREST has been spotted on PENN COMMON and in a MERRY HILL garden.

Mammals which can be found in and around the town include PIPISTRELLE and LONG EARED BATS, FOXES, BADGERS, GREY SQUIRRELS, HEDGEHOGS, RABBITS, MOLES, VOLES and SHREWS as well as the more common and less welcome HOUSE MOUSE and BROWN RAT. The rarest mammal sighting of all has been that of a MUNTJAC, a small deer introduced from CHINA which was struck by a car, but survived, in TETTENHALL in 1976.

THE COMMON FROG, TOAD and SMOOTH NEWT are widespread in Wolverhampton and have even occurred in RAKEGATE WOOD,and OXLEY. The largest and rarest newt, THE GREAT CRESTED, occurs in a few places , such as the ponds at HADLEY'S BRICKYARDS and a neglected gardenpool at CLAREGATE.

THE COMMA, a butterfly that once became scarce in Britain is present in small numbers to the SOUTH and WEST of the town and one of the smallest butterflies, the GREEN HAIRSTREAK exists on PENN COMMON.

The ORANGE TIP and DINGY SKIPPER live on the COMMON and the LIME HAWK MOTH, POPLAR, EYED and ELEPHANT HAWKS are found in and around the town.

The caterpillar of the CINNABAR MOTH wears the same black and gold colours as Wolverhampton Wanderers FC and has been seen in BUSHBURY and in DARLINGTON STREET, not far from MOLYNEUX.

THE SIX-SPOT BURNET lives in colonies around the town and the BROWN HAWKER DRAGONFLY inhabits the BIRMINGHAM CANAL off BROAD STREET, VALLEY PARK, BRADMORE and PENN and the smaller COMMON DARTER can be seen around garden ponds and industrial watercourses.

WASPS, BEES and other insects are, of course, indigenous but the town also hosts the KNOPPER GALL - a small gall-wasp and the HOLLY GALL MIDGE.

The wildlife of Wolverhampton is being conserved and monitored by THE STAFFORDSHIRE NATURE CONSERVATION TRUST, 30a WINDMILL LANE, CASTLECROFT, WOLVERHAMPTON.

MISCELLANEOUS

Wolverhampton possesses 10 grade 11 (Special interest) Listed Buildings and 142 Grade 11 (interest).

The first female councillor was Labour's Emma Sprosan.

The town has more than 450 clubs and societies covering interests varying from Angling to archery, bats, bees and beermats, caving, canals,chess and charities, conservation, cribbage and cricket, dogs, dancing and drama, embroidery, ex-service and first aid, TV , tennis and transport.

There are 13 Townswomen's Guilds, five tennis clubs, a Dr WHO Society and a "Six of One Club" formed as an appreciation of the TV series "The Prisoner".

The United Kingdom Spoon Collectors Club is represented in Wolverhampton along with two stamp collecting clubs and more than 20 organisations and clubs for senior citizens.

There are almost 20 clubs, societies and choirs for music, a Literary Society, 15 historical societies and three golf clubs.

Each year about 800 full time students and 7000 part time students register with Wulfrun College which has over 170 teaching staff. Last year over 100 students went on to university or polytechnic.

Wulfrun College has almost 30 GCSE subjects to choose from and a full range of 'A' level courses including Psychology, the sciences, languages and arts.

The first cycle race in Wolverhampton was won by Dan Rudge on a cycle he built himself.

The Queen Mother is honorary governor of Wolverhampton Grammar School.

The Polytechnic has launched a one year BA (Hons) Business Enterprise course for entrepreneurs.

Queen Square in 1894

Industrial property prices start at about £2 a square foot.

There were a total of 70 members of the Small Business Club when it celebrated its first anniversary.

Wolverhampton is the sixteenth largest shopping centre in the country.

The Council is the biggest employer in the town.

The town is a sportsman's paradise with Racing, Athletics, Speedway, Hockey, Cricket and Soccer given national prominence.

Wolverhampton Wanderers were formed in 1887 and was known as the Goldthorn Football Club. The club, a founder member of the Football League turned professional in 1888. The club became the first team to become champions of all four English League Division in 1988 when they were top of Division Four.

Wolves players *(and club officials)* who brought the Cup back to the Midlands in 1893. *Back Row (l ro r)* - R. Baugh, Mr. A. Hollingworth *(chairman)*, J. Lewis *(director)*, A. Blackham *(linesman)*, H. Allen. *Middle* - R. Topham, W. Malpass, W. C. Rose, G. Swift, G. Kinsey. *Front* - D. Wykes, J. Butcher, H. Wood, A. Griffin and Mr. J. H. Addenbrooke *(sec-manager)*.

A row between two water companies, one owned by Wolverhampton and the other private was settled in favour of the private one by Parliament and almost resulted in the town being made bankrupt around 1855.

The proceedings in the Parliamentary committee to decide who should supply the town with water cost the Corporation £6,500 in legal charges. A hastily called meeting of residents denied liability and told the council to get itself out of trouble. Creditors issued writs and whilst the council was considering the predicament the bailiffs appeared in the Town Hall. The furniture of the town hall down to the town clerk's pen were seized as were the helmets, handcuffs, uniforms and even beds at the Police Barracks. The fire engine followed to the delight of the bailiffs and citizens who reviled the council and jeered at the impotent police. It is said only self interest prevented them from setting fire to their homes to see what would happen. A meeting designed to appeal for a special rate to avert the crisis endorsed the general opinion that the councillors should be left to stew and ended with a hearty rendering of "Rule Britannia".

Members of the Wolverhampton Council were even afraid to go to Birmingham where they were a laughing stock. The bailiffs who had been temporarily bought off by a payment from the Magistrate's Fee Fund, appeared again, seized the market and impounded the dues on all livestock taken there for sale. The ratepayers were refusing to pay their rates and the market was practically the only source of income left. It couldn't get worse, but it did when the Town Clerk quit and presented his own bill of £2,034 for out-of-pocket expenses in fighting the Water Company.

The town was in dire straights but just when all seemed lost the Mayor Edward Peel accompanied the rate collector around the town and the citizens, now ready to pay for their fun, one by one agreed to pay an extra voluntary rate of one shilling in the pound.

The whole issue ended happily and even the London engineer who issued the writ that started the whole comedy off subscribed £100 towards the voluntary rate.

Prince Consort Statue